LED ZEPPELIN

While I was searching through the archives for visual and audio material for the Led Zeppelin DVD, I re-discovered these 1972 performances from the 25th June, LA Forum and 27th June, Long Beach Arena. This is Led Zeppelin at its best and an illustration of *How The West Was Won*.

Jimmy Page, London, March 2003

HOW THE WEST WAS WON

Project Manger: Carol Cuellar
Book Art Layout: Joe Klucar
Album Cover Art: © 2003 Atlantic Recording Corporation

CONTENTS

HEARTBREAKER

Words and Music by
JIMMY PAGE, ROBERT PLANT,
JOHN PAUL JONES and JOHN BONHAM

Moderately ♩ = 98

Heartbreaker - 5 - 1
PFM0321

Peo - ple talk - in' all a - round__ 'bout the way you left me__ flat.__

I don't care__ what the peo - ple say,__ I know where their jive__ is at.

One thing I do have on my mind__ if you could clar - i - fy, please__ do. It's the

6

way you call__ me an-oth-er guy's name when I try to make love to

you,__ yeah.__

N.C.

Free tempo solo

Heartbreaker - 5 - 4
PFM0321

Verse 2:
Well, it's been ten years and maybe more since I first set eyes on you.
The best years of my life gone by. Here I am alone and blue.
Some people cry and some people die by the wicked ways of love.
But I'll just keep rollin' along with the grace of the Lord above.

Verse 3:
Work so hard I can't unwind, get some money saved,
Abuse my love a thousand times, however hard I try.
Heartbreaker, your time has come, can't take your evil ways.
Go away, you heartbreaker.

IMMIGRANT SONG

Words and Music by
JIMMY PAGE and ROBERT PLANT

ah.

1. I come from the land of the ice and snow, from the mid - night sun where the hot springs flow.
come from the land of the ice and snow, from the mid - night sun where the hot springs flow.

Immigrant Song - 4 - 1
PFM0321

10

11

Immigrant Song - 4 - 4
PFM0321

BLACK DOG

Words and Music by
JIMMY PAGE, ROBERT PLANT
and JOHN PAUL JONES

* Vocal sung 1 octave higher.

14

Verses 2 & 4:

2. I got-ta roll, can't stand still,___ got a flam-in' heart,___ can't

4. *See additional lyrics*

get my fill.___

N.C.

cue notes 2nd time only

Eyes that shine,___ burn-in' red,___ dreams of you___ all

can't you do me   now?__
while you do me   now.__

Hey__

3. Did-n't

ah.

Verse 3:
Didn't take too long 'fore I found out what
People mean by down and out.

Spent my money, took my car ,
Started tellin' her friends she gonna be a star.

I don't know, but I been told,
A big-legged woman ain't got no soul.
(To Chorus:)

Verse 4:
All I ask for, all I pray,
Steady loaded woman gonna come my way.

Need a woman gonna hold my hand
Will tell me no lies, make me a happy man.
Ah ah ah ah ah ah ah ah ah ah ah ah ah.
(To Coda)

OVER THE HILLS AND FAR AWAY

Words and Music by
JIMMY PAGE and ROBERT PLANT

Man - y have_ I loved_ and man - y times_ been bit - ten.
Man - y times_ I've lied,_ and man - y times_ I've list-ened.

Man - y times_ I've gazed_____ a - long the o - pen road._
Man - y times_ I've won - dered how much there is to know._

(Guitar)

22

N.C.

Repeat as desired for solo

(Harmony guitar)

24

Man-y is___ a word that on - ly leaves you guess-in', a-

guess - in' 'bout a thing you real - ly ought to know,___

SINCE I'VE BEEN LOVING YOU

Words and Music by
JIMMY PAGE, ROBERT PLANT
and JOHN PAUL JONES

Slow blues ♩. = 42

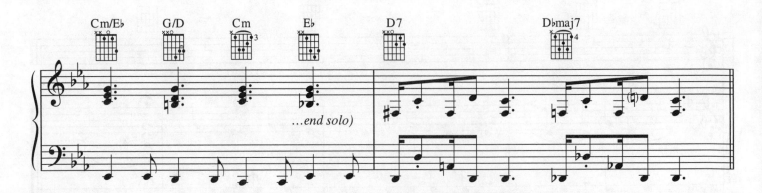

Since I've Been Loving You - 6 - 1
PFM0321

Since I've Been Loving You - 6 - 5
PFM0321

Verse 2:
Everybody's trying to tell me
That you didn't mean me no good.
I've been trying, Lord, let me tell you.
Let me tell you I really did the best I could.
I've been working from seven to eleven every night.
It kinda makes my life a drag.
Lord, you know it ain't right.
Since I've been loving you,
I'm about to lose my worried mind.

Verse 3:
Guitar solo ad lib.
(To Bridge:)

Verse 4:
Do you remember, mama, when I knocked upon your door?
I said you had the nerve to tell me you didn't want me no more.
I open my front door, hearing my back door slam.
You must have one of them new-fangled back door man.
I've been working from seven to eleven every night.
It kinda makes my life a drag.
Ah, yeah, it makes it a drag.
Baby, since I've been loving you,
I'm about to lose my worried mind.
(To Coda)

Since I've Been Loving You - 6 - 6
PFM0321

STAIRWAY TO HEAVEN

Words and Music by
JIMMY PAGE and ROBERT PLANT

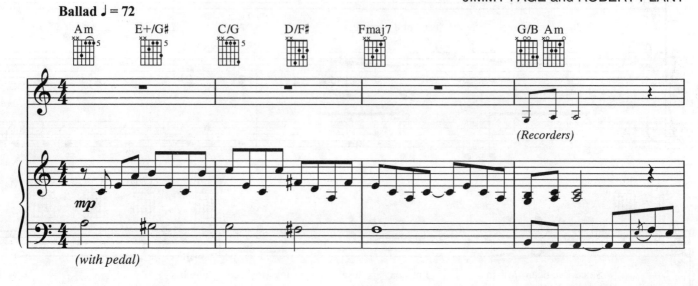

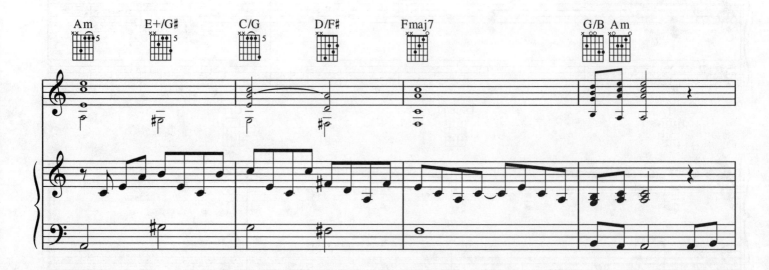

38

Verses 2 & 3:
C G/B Am C G/B Fmaj7
feel - ing I get_ when I look to the west,_ and my spir - it is cry - ing for leav -
whis - pered that soon_ if we all call the tune,_ then the pip - er will lead us to rea -
Am C G/B Am
ing. In my thoughts I have seen_ rings of smoke through the trees,___ and the
son. And a new day will dawn,_ for those who stand long,___ and the
3
C G/B Fmaj7 Am C G/B
voic - es of those who stand look - ing.
for - ests will ech - o with laugh - ter.
Am7 Dsus D Am7 Em/D
Ooh,___ it makes me won - der.

there's still time to change_the road_ you're on._
your stair - way lies on the_ whis - 'prin' wind._

And it makes me won - der,

ahh._____

41

Repeat as desired for solo

solo continues

And as we wind_ on down the road,___ our shad-ow's tall - er than our soul.__

Stairway to Heaven - 10 - 8
PFM0321

GOING TO CALIFORNIA

Gtr. tuned in "Double Drop D":
⑥ = D   ③ = G
⑤ = A   ② = B
④ = D   ① = D

Words and Music by
JIMMY PAGE and ROBERT PLANT

Moderate folk ballad ♩ = 76

1. Spend my days___ with a wom-an un-kind,___ Smoked my stuff___ and
3. *See additional lyrics*

drank___ all my wine.___

46

Instrumental Bridge:

To Coda

Going to California - 7 - 3
PFM0321

Verse 3:
Find a queen without a king,
They say she plays guitar and cries and sings, la-la-la-la.
Ride a white mare in the footsteps of dawn,
Tryin' to find a woman who's never, never, never been born.
Standin' on a hill in the mountain of dreams,
Tellin' myself it's not as hard, hard, hard as it seems.
Mm-mm, now.
(To Coda)

BRON-YR-AUR STOMP

Gtr. tuned in "Open D":
⑥ = D ③ = F#
⑤ = A ② = A
④ = D ① = D
Capoed at 3 fr.

Words and Music by
JIMMY PAGE, ROBERT PLANT
and JOHN PAUL JONES

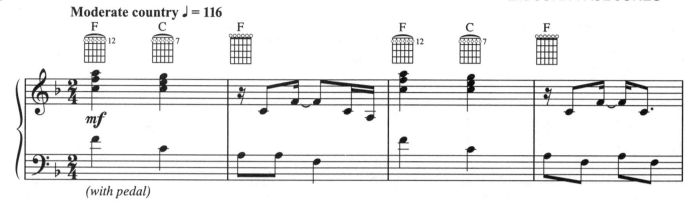

(with pedal)

Bron-Yr-Aur Stomp - 7 - 1
PFM0321

Play 3 times

Harmony line 2nd and 3rd time only.

Bron-Yr-Aur Stomp - 7 - 3
PFM0321

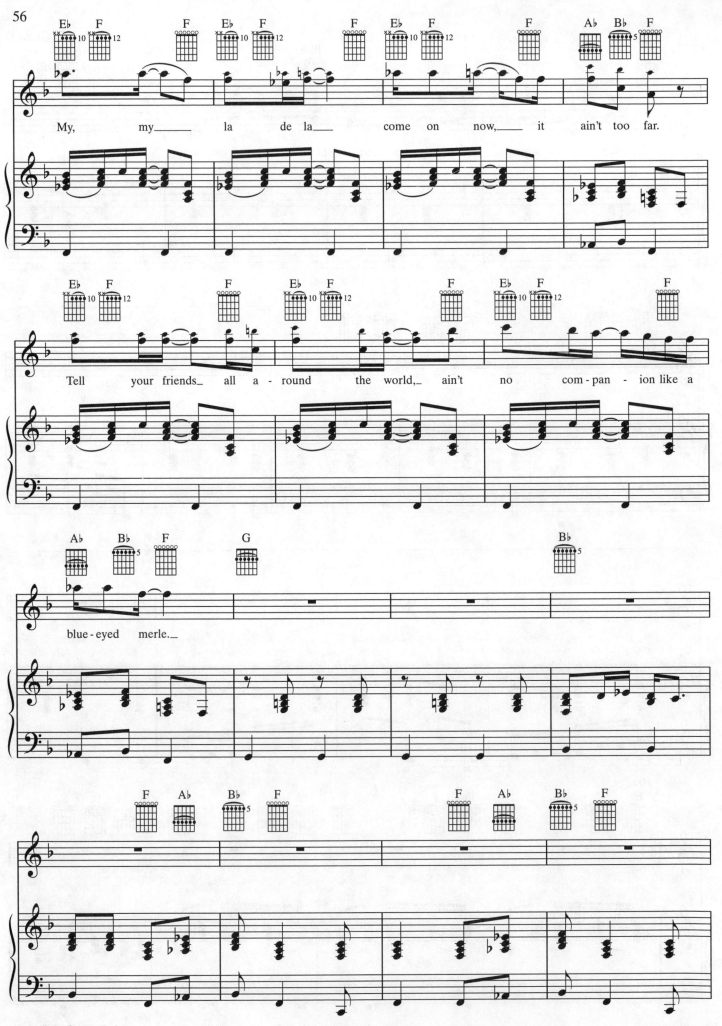

D.C. al Coda

Verse 2:
Well, if the sun shines so bright,
Or our way is darkest night,
The road we choose is always right, so fine.
Ah, can a love be so strong
When so many loves go wrong?
Will our love go on and on and on and on and on.
(To Chorus:)

Verse 3:
So of one thing I am sure,
It's a friendship so pure,
Angels singing all around my door so fine.
Yeah, ain't but one thing to do,
Spend my natural life with you,
You're the finest dog I knew, so find.

Chorus 3:
When you're old and your eyes are dim.
There ain't no old shep gonna happen again.
We'll still go walking down country lanes,
I'll sing the same old song, hear me call your name.

THAT'S THE WAY

Gtr. tuned in "Open G":
⑥ = D ③ = G
⑤ = G ② = B
④ = D ① = D

Words and Music by
JIMMY PAGE and ROBERT PLANT

Moderately ♩ = 96

Verses 1, 2, 4, & 5:

1. I don't know how I'm gon-na tell you   I can't play with you no

2. 4. 5. *See additional lyrics*

more.   I don't know how I'm gon-na   do what ma-ma told me,

* Original recording in G♭.

That's the Way - 6 - 1
PFM0321

62

Verse 2:
I can't believe what people saying,
You're gonn let your hair hang down.
I'm satisfied to sit here working all day long,
You're in the darkest side of town.
(To Verse 3:)

Verse 4:
And yesterday I saw you standing by the river,
And weren't those tears that filled your eyes?
And all the fish that lay in dirty water dying,
Had they got you hypnotized?

Verse 5:
And yesterday I saw you kissing tiny flowers,
But all that lives is born to die.
And so I say to you that nothing really matters,
And all you do is stand and cry.

Verse 6:
I don't know what to say about it,
When all your ears have turned away.
But now's the time to look and look again at what you see,
Is this the way it ought to stay?
(To Chorus:)

DAZED AND CONFUSED

Words and Music by
JIMMY PAGE

Moderately slow ♩. = 52

N.C.

Verse 1:

1. Been dazed and con - fused__ for so long, it's not true. A -

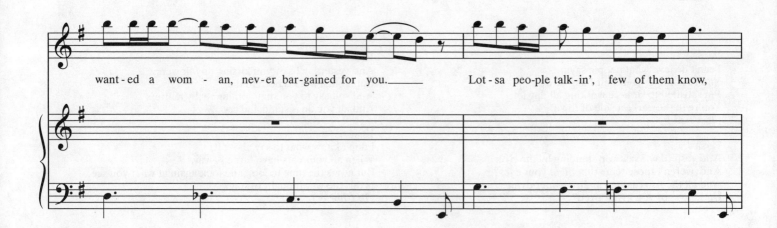

want - ed a wom - an, nev - er bar - gained for you.___ Lot - sa peo - ple talk - in', few of them know,

Dazed and Confused - 8 - 1
PFM0321

Oh,_____ yeah,_____ al -

right._____

Ah.   Ah.   Ah.   Ah.

69

Guitar Solo: (Play as desired)

Dazed and Confused - 8 - 6
PFM0321

70

Verse 3:
Every day I work so hard, bringin' home my hard-earned pay.
Try to love you, baby, but you push me away.
Don't know where you're goin', only know just where you've been.
Sweet little baby, I want you again.
(To Instrumental Bridge:)

Verse 4:
Been dazed and confused for so long, it's not true.
Wanted a woman, never bargained for you.
Take it easy, baby, let them say what they will.
Tongue wag so much when I send you the bill, oh, yeah, alright.
(To Outro:)

WHAT IS AND WHAT SHOULD NEVER BE

Words and Music by
JIMMY PAGE and ROBERT PLANT

74

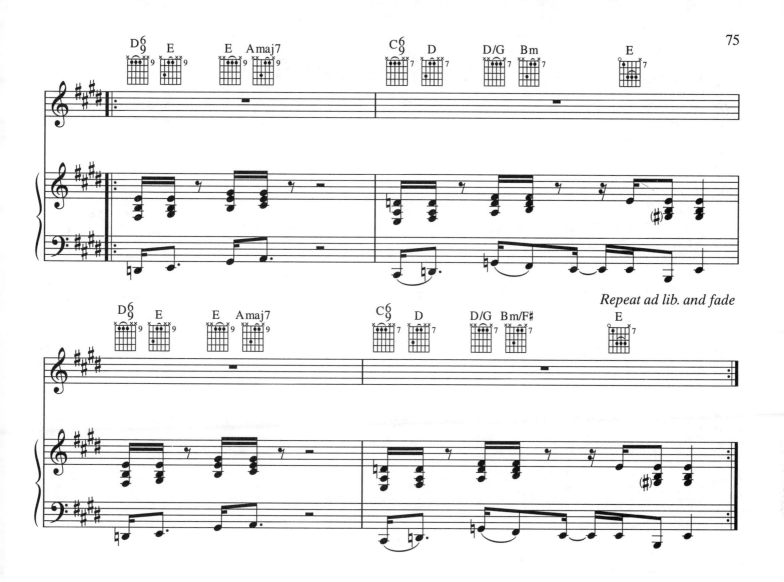

Repeat ad lib. and fade

Verse 2:
And if you say to me tomorrow,
Oh, what fun it all would be.
Then what's to stop us pretty baby
But what is and what should never be.
(To Chorus:)

Verse & Chorus 3:
Instrumental

Verse 4:
So if you wake up with the sunrise
And all your dreams are still as new.
And happiness is what you need so bad,
Girl, the answer lies with you, yeah.
(To Chorus:)

What Is and What Should Never Be - 4 - 4
PFM0321

DANCING DAYS

Gtr. tuned in "Open G":
⑥ = D ③ = G
⑤ = G ②ﾠ= B
④ = D ①ﾠ= D

Words and Music by
JIMMY PAGE and ROBERT PLANT

Moderate rock ♩ = 116

(8vb throughout)

Verses 1 & 3:

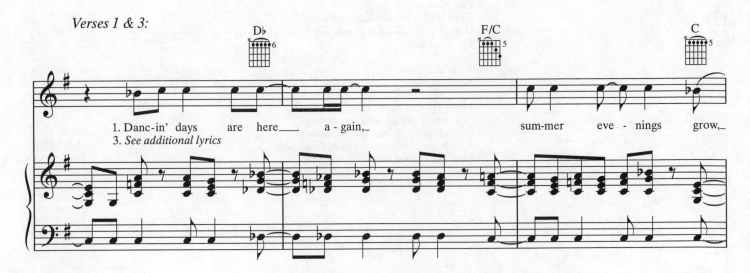

1. Danc-in' days are here___ a-gain,_ sum-mer eve-nings grow,_
3. *See additional lyrics*

Dancing Days - 5 - 1
PFM0321

Verse 3:
You told your mama I'd get you home
But you didn't say that I got no car.
I saw a lion, he was standin' alone
With tadpole in a jar.

Chorus 3:
You know it's alright, I said, it's alright,
I guess it's all in my heart, heart, heart.
You'll be my only, my one and only.
Is that the way it should start?

Verse 4:
Said, dancin' days are here again
As the summer evenings grow.
You are my flower, you are my power,
You are my woman who knows.

Chorus 4:
I said, it's alright, y'know it's alright,
You know it's all in my heart.
You'll be my only, yes, my one and only, yes.
Is that the way it should start?
I know it isn't.
(To Interude:)

MOBY DICK

Music by
JOHN BONHAM, JOHN PAUL JONES
and JIMMY PAGE

Moderately ♩ = 96

* N.C.

* Guitar: Tune ⑥ = D

Moby Dick - 3 - 1
PFM0321

82

(Guitar fills)

(Guitar fills)

(Guitar fills)

(Guitar fills)

8vb--

8vb------------

Moby Dick - 3 - 2
PFM0321

Free Drum Solo

(Drum fills)

(Drum fills)

Moby Dick - 3 - 3
PFM0321

83

ROCK AND ROLL

Words and Music by
JIMMY PAGE, ROBERT PLANT,
JOHN PAUL JONES and JOHN BONHAM

Ooh, yeah, ooh,___ yeah.___ Ooh, yeah,

ooh,___ yeah.___ It's been a long time, been a long time, been a long,

lone - ly, lone - ly, lone - ly, lone - ly, lone - ly time

(Drum solo, free tempo)

Verse 2:
It's been a long time since the book of love.
I can't count the tears of a life with no love.
A-carry me back, carry me back, carry me back
Mm, baby, where I come from, whoa-whoa, whoa-oh-oh-ho.
It's been a long time, been a long time
Been a long, lonely, lonely, lonely, lonely, lonely time.
Ah, ah-ah, ah-ah.
(To Guitar Solo:)

Verse 3:
Oh, it seems so long since we walked in the moonlight
A-makin' vows that just couldn't work right.
Haw, yeah, open your arms, open your arms, open your arms
Baby, let my love come running in, a-yeah.
It's been a long time, been a long time
Been a long, lonely, lonely, lonely, lonely, lonely time.
(To Outro:)

THE OCEAN

Words and Music by
JOHN BONHAM, JOHN PAUL JONES,
JIMMY PAGE and ROBERT PLANT

The Ocean - 5 - 1
PFM0321

Got no___ time to pack my bag,___ my foots out - side the door.___

I got a date, I can't_ be late_ for the hell - hound hai - la ball.___

2nd time: Guitar solo ad lib.

Verse 2:
Singin' to an ocean, I can hear the ocean's roar.
Play for free, I play for me, I play a whole lot more, more.
Singin' 'bout the good things and the sun that lights the day.
I used to sing to the mountains, has the ocean lost its way?

Verse 3:
Sitting 'round singing songs 'til the night turns into day.
Used to sing to the mountains but the mountains washed away.
Now I'm singing all my songs to the girl who won my heart.
She is only three years old and it's a real fine way to start.

BRING IT ON HOME

Words and Music by
WILLIE DIXON

Repeat as desired

Bring It On Home - 7 - 1
PFM0321

watch out, watch out.

Slower ♩ = 100 (♫ = ♫)
N.C.

Bridge:

Try to tell___ you, babe,___ what you try - in' to do?___

2.3.4. See additional lyrics

Try-in' to love___ me, ba - by, love some oth - er man too.___ Well, bring it on

home, bring it on home. home,___ bring it back

home._   Bring it back home   to me, ba - by.

Tempo I

Bring it on home,___ bring it on___home to you.___

Bridge 2:
Went a litlle walk downtown,
Messed and got back late.
Found a note there waiting,
It said, "Daddy, I just can't wait."
Bring it on home, *etc.*

Bridge 3:
Tell you, pretty baby,
You love to mess me 'roun'.
I'm gonna give you lovin', baby.
Gonna move you out o' town.
Bring it on home, *etc.*

Bridge 4:
Sweetest little baby
Daddy ever saw.
I'm gonna give you lovin',
I'm gonna give you more.
Bring it on home, *etc.*

WHOLE LOTTA LOVE

Words and Music by
JIMMY PAGE, ROBERT PLANT,
JOHN PAUL JONES and JOHN BONHAM

Moderately ♩ = 92

1. You__ need

Verse:

cool - in',__ ba - by, I'm not fool - in'.__ I'm gon - na

2.3. *See additional lyrics*

106

Repeat ad lib. and fade

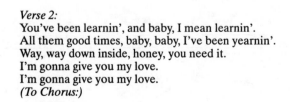

Verse 2:
You've been learnin', and baby, I mean learnin'.
All them good times, baby, baby, I've been yearnin'.
Way, way down inside, honey, you need it.
I'm gonna give you my love.
I'm gonna give you my love.
(To Chorus:)

Verse 3:
You've been coolin', baby, I've been droolin'.
All the good times, baby, I've been misusin'.
Way, way down inside, I'm gonna give you my love.
I'm gonna give you every inch of my love.
Gonna give you my love.
(To Chorus:)

Whole Lotta Love - 5 - 5
PFM0321